Joyful Journey

A guide back to the wild self

Gia Lulic

First paperback edition September 2022

Editor: Ana H De La Vega
Book cover design by Sonal R Vagadia
Interior book design by Henrietta Sampson

ISBN 978-1-3999-3439-8 (paperback)

ACKNOWLEDGEMENTS

One of the many important lessons which the process of writing this book has reinforced for me is that whatever journey toward extraordinary we find ourselves on, we will not be on it alone. There will be people around us who encourage us, support us and most importantly (and perhaps above all else) wholeheartedly believe in us. I want to acknowledge everyone who has been instrumental in making the dream of publishing this message my reality. My divine parents, whose unconditional support and love I've always had. My mother especially, who would move mountains for me should the need ever arise and my very talented brother who encouraged me to publish the text. To my two incredible soul sisters and family away from home who have been my greatest teachers, cheerleaders, and inspirers. Thank you for always sharing the hype but also keeping me in line. My brilliant colleague and friend who gave me the final nudge to publish the text and whose lovely wife offered incredible generosity by designing my cover. My amazing editor who came to my rescue at the very moment that I needed her, unprompted and unplanned. To my beautiful friends from home who shaped me in ways that I cannot begin to unpick and the rest of my chosen family in London whose strength, generosity and relentlessly wicked sense of humour have always reminded me to keep my spirit light.

CONTENTS

This text is dedicated to the wild child that lingers in us all, yet has been silenced, ignored, or neglected. Our wild child is the pure part of us all that cannot be defined, explained nor contained. It is the mystery that holds within it the potential for all human experience. We feel its presence in every moment of joy we have experienced and every impassioned thought that has ever crossed our minds.

Read this text with an open heart and you will feel the wild child take over, even if only for a moment. This one ray of light will reveal to you open doors to new possibilities. Act on the ideas immediately, in any small way; or at the very least, write them down. They will be your clues leading you to a life that you can only imagine from your present state. Little by little you will let go of control and let the wild child take the reins. Your mind may not understand this, but I trust that your heart will: *You* are the masterpiece. *You* are the solution. *You* are the purpose.

> "In its proper and healthy state, the wild self is not docile or vacuous. It Is alert and responsive to any given movement or moment. It is not locked into an absolute and repetitive pattern for any and all circumstances. It has creative choice."
> Clarissa Pinkola Estés, *Women Who Run with the Wolves*

INTRODUCTION

The sound of the alarm startled me awake and I jumped up in my bed. Even after years of being jolted awake by that shrilling noise, my body never quite learned to embrace it. I had tried every tune available but would still end up wanting to hurl my phone across the room. I told myself to accept this, that I was just not a morning person, but I knew the opposite was true – my dear mother never stopped reminding me how as a baby I would wake up wearing a big smile (which apparently is not the norm).

Recently though, I was finding it more and more difficult to accept having to do anything that did not match who I had become. This included my desk job, which was steadily becoming unbearable at best, and some form of mild torture at worst. I suspected this inner rebellion also had something to do with the anxiety symptoms I had developed earlier that year. This experience taught me that going against oneself for a prolonged period catches up.

Unfortunately, honouring the 'shoulds' seemed to be the unofficial benchmark of a life well lived, with everyone around me following the well-trodden path of finishing school, working the nine-to-five grind, buying a house and saving for retirement. While there is nothing wrong with this neat timeline, and all other rigid structures imposed by culture, society and family, I reject this as the standard way to spend our life. Even as an adolescent, I couldn't compute the paradox of being individuals with unique perspectives and talents, yet all being encouraged to follow the same worn-out journey. As an adult, I have witnessed enough people around me experiencing a mid-life crisis to conclude that there is something very screwy and unnatural about the way societal norms have set us up to live our lives.

To those who follow this timeline naturally and wholeheartedly: keep doing what you're doing. However, if you're like me, and a witness to yourself following this formula heartlessly in an attempt to be "secure", you will probably end up unfulfilled and numb to the magic that is this life experience.

By this stage in my life, my spirit and body have agreed that this will not be my path. No matter how scary this decision was, I could no longer avoid making it. I was forced to admit what I have known all along: that I am a freedom seeker, a sovereign being, too connected to myself to follow a schedule that has been drawn up for me. What inspired me to write this book is my conviction that you too are a freedom seeker.

As children, we wake up eager to search for ways to squeeze the most joy and fun out of our day. We view the world through a sense of wonder and live in it as though it's our very own playground, where self-expression is our only guiding force. However, as we get older, the 'shoulds' start to take over our life – first imposed by family or society, and eventually and worst of all, by ourselves.

My intention for this book is to set myself free from the conditioning that has led to this daily grind and in doing so, to set you free also. By sharing the wisdom I have collected in my own life and borrowed from those who appear to be peaceful and satisfied in theirs, I hope to inspire you too. I intend to give you the nudge to leap unreservedly towards that which you truly dream of doing and thus restore your spirit to what it was when you were a child.

Like me, I believe you have a wealth of experience and knowledge that is exclusively yours and equally valuable to us all. My wish is that you find a way to unleash this unique, never-before-witnessed perspective to enrich the world, and in the process, make your own life the fulfilling joyride it was always meant to be. We each have our channels for self-expression. Whether it's painting, dancing, singing, writing, speaking, all the above, or something else altogether, I hope this book will inspire you to start doing what has always been natural to you.

This journey, like many great ones, starts in London. I see London as the global capital, so it's a perfect fit for me as I like to think of myself as a citizen of the world. After my family and I left former Yugoslavia in 1993 to live in Australia, we moved to various parts of Europe, changing homes thirty-five times. The idea of a physical home was a foreign concept, and the experience of moving around became my norm – until I moved to London. There was something about the energy of this collection of villages, each unique in its spirit, home to free thinkers, dreamers, Peter Pans and artists of the world. I had never witnessed so many contradictory realities coexisting side by side: the old world with the new world, the chaotic with the peaceful, the alternative with the straight and narrow, the have-nots alongside the abundant, the joyful and inspired with those in despair. It could be your utopia or your dystopia.

London was a place where one could belong to any of these realities from one day to another, or as I did, to all of them at once. Once I embraced its terrifying enchantment, the city opened its arms to me like an old friend. For once in my life, the comfort-seeking part of me had found a place to peacefully co-exist with the perpetual nomad in me. I felt an unprecedented sense of freedom to be my child-like self, to live my days in wonder and reinvent myself as many times as I pleased. I saw doors that were wide open for me to walk or run through at every turn.

And so, London became the first place that felt like home. As I realise now, there are no coincidences in life, and we are innately pulled (willingly or not) towards that which is the truest reflection of who we are. From the day I stepped off that plane at Heathrow Airport I felt like the energy of the city was somehow that true reflection of something in me.

Shortly before deciding to make my move to London, a close friend and I had an unusually serious conversation (which in Australia we fondly refer to as 'a deep and meaningful') over wine, where she confirmed my nagging fear that my life didn't at all reflect who I was, and who she knew me to be. I was taken aback by this confession but was also relieved and touched that my friend had observed this and put it so eloquently. I realised two things that day: one, that only a true friend dares to hold up a mirror so that we are in full view of our shortcomings. The other is that perhaps true success is not at all what we've been taught, but something as simple as having the world we create around us reflect that which is truest and therefore greatest in us.

I believe we are all born with this knowledge. In this manifesto, I offer you and me practices and philosophies that are both spiritual and practical, alongside non-painful and in-the-flow exercises to help you explore and ground your inner wild child. Most of all, I aspire to permit you to wear yourself with pride. I hope we will all be led to rediscover parts of ourselves we have forgotten and neglected, so we can regain our true status as creators and partake in a life that is a true reflection of our innate greatness.

SECTION 1: DISCOVERING OUR ESSENCE

FOLLOWING OUR JOY AND SENSE OF PEACE

Writer Joseph Campbell said to follow our bliss. I would like to add to his wise words and encourage us all to follow our peace. Many people associate bliss with the feeling of happiness which, as we have all discovered, is fleeting. Peace, as I understand it, is entirely different. The feeling of peace can be found in various sentiments, such as feeling interested, content, clear-minded, appreciative, playful, invincible, serene, and even sad. Unlike happiness, peace is unwavering. It is an integral knowledge that all is well, irrespective of how it looks on the outside.

It is not a state we can necessarily cultivate, but rather peace is something that comes about when we act in a way that is true to who we are. People who act on their truth may spend their whole life being challenged by their environment but will remain peaceful through it all. Nelson Mandela, Martin Luther King, Mahatma Gandhi and Joan of Arc are a few examples of figures whose lives seemed full of turbulence and resistance, yet the message that emanated from each one of them was one of peace and unity.

If you've ever had the great fortune of being in a peaceful state for a prolonged period, you will know its profound power. From my own experience, the things that bring about a deep sense of peace have served as breadcrumbs to finding the people and things that are the truest reflection of who I am and who I wish to become. Some clues are obvious, such as an eagerness for travelling or an interest in studying history, while others cannot be defined so easily. It is no secret that the most successful people love what they do. However, most of us struggle to figure out what this is, which is why it's so important to follow the little clues about what brings us peace.

For the longest time, I assumed that the sense of peace I derived from having deep conversations with friends was completely unrelated to a fulfilling career. With so many self-made podcast gurus out there who have made a career out of talking to inspiring and interesting people, I now realise how wrong I was. We live in rapidly evolving times, where self-expression of any kind has never been so abundant and celebrated. The wild world of social media, the internet, and platforms like YouTube, for all its perceived mishaps, has provided an opportunity to set us all free in a way that no one could have predicted. With as little as a decent internet connection, we each have the platform from which to broadcast our contribution to the world at our fingertips. For those of us fortunate enough to have our primary needs met, life has never held more potential to be that playground we sought out as children.

Let us write a list of things that make us feel peaceful, clear, and at one with the world and ourselves. What are things we do that get us out of our heads? Let us focus on a time when we've experienced that feeling of pure presence that makes everything else temporarily irrelevant. This exercise should be approached with an open heart. Now is the time to throw assumptions and limitations out the window and list everything that comes to mind, no matter how random it sounds.

____

____

____

WHAT'S HAPPENING WITH OUR ENERGY?

Assuming there are many of us who are not sure what we would like out of life, the following section and exercises will help us get a step closer to finding out.

While for some of us, our passion is obvious – we may have dedicated our entire life to our love for dance so there is little mystery around what a fulfilling future looks like – for others like myself, working out my true path has been more of a process of elimination. I had many things I felt excited about, but not one that stuck out enough for me to know it was the one to pursue. I first had to go down several paths and hit a dead end to realise they were the wrong ones for me.

The clues to our passion lie in the activities and people that leave us feeling energised, as opposed to those that leave us feeling drained and empty. The energy I gained from discussing politics, existentialist ideas and world views may not have been obvious signs in determining my direction, but it provided a contrast to those things that left me feeling lifeless – in my case, jobs where I felt emotionally and spiritually drained. It is one thing to feel tired and satisfied and a whole other to feel emotionally depleted. As someone who is naturally joyful and full of energy, it is blindingly obvious when I am not in my element to both myself and to everyone around me. As a result, some of my best days have been those where I finally got up the nerve to quit my job or had the good fortune of being fired.

When we are not sure where to head, we can practice becoming aware of our energy levels following certain interactions and situations. This is also helpful as it will not allow us to go too far with something we are pursuing or someone we are interacting with.

For example, following a series of interactions with a person, I will look out for a pattern on whether my energy is lifted, remains unchanged, or is drained after I have walked away from each conversation. If I observe that my energy is consistently being weakened, I take a moment to look deeper into why that might be and usually find it is because I give more than I am receiving back. Being surrounded by certain people or situations that are depleting our energy will inevitably weaken our being. Ideally, we should strive to get to a place where most people we choose to make time for are those who elevate our energy and therefore leave us feeling stronger.

Considering this idea, I ask us to go through our weekly activities and get honest about the level of energy we gain from doing these. We can also wish to do the same for our interactions with the people in our life. This exercise is not about encouraging you to quit your job, end friendships or cut off relationships, but instead, it's about taking inventory and becoming acutely aware of which parts of our experience align with our intuitive selves. Rating our level of energy from 1 to 10 after each experience will give us a clear indication of where we might wish to make changes, and at the very least which activities or interactions can safely be eliminated from our life.

DISCOVERING THE CORE DRIVE

I once had a long conversation with my mum about my childhood in former Yugoslavia. I discovered that the driving force that inspired my actions as a child is the same as that which inspires my actions as an adult. According to my mum's recollection of our beachside holidays camping in Croatia, I would sneak off and go into other people's tents and ask them questions about where they came from. I was fascinated that people spoke different languages and longed to know more about their worlds. This curiosity about people who I perceived to be different from me, coupled with my need for novelty and adventure, was just as prominent then as it is now.

A few years back, a close friend gave me a birthday card with a picture of a little girl climbing on top of a kitchen counter and peeking inside one of the cabinet doors. My mum commented on many occasions that if a single picture could capture my essence, it would be that one. Forever searching, wandering, and blissfully oblivious to the rules most people never think to question, much less break.

The significance of discovering what drives us cannot be overstated in our quest for freedom and creating an extraordinary life. I believe each of us comes here with a particular theme or drive that shows itself very early on. What did you love to do as a child? What were some of the patterns or quirks parents and caregivers remember about your behaviour as a child? Furthermore, what are common defining attributes and trends that friends notice about you? If we can establish what these are, it will bring us closer to our true essence by providing clues about what truly fascinates us and so drives our actions.

UNCOVERING THE 'WHY'

It is important to know the 'why' for what we choose to pour our time and energy into. In this chapter, we will understand how important it is to emotionally resonate with the reasons we have identified for ourselves.

It has become commonplace to observe people who have experienced unprecedented levels of success in their chosen field but still struggle with depression. While it plays a big role, success in just one area of our life does not necessarily lead us to peace or to thrive.

Meaning takes precedent over success in contributing to fulfilment in our chosen endeavours. For people like self-development master Tony Robbins, meaning and success clearly overlap, and he like many others has thrived largely because he has combined the two. However, this is not always the case. For example, society ranks people according to their "net worth". This is what we hear over and over and so become conditioned to value financial success as a path to freedom and fulfilment. After all, we all have a need to be validated and seen, so it is easy to confuse this for our sole meaning and contribution. Many unconsciously value work that will bring most financial abundance, status and popularity, and so forget to consider what cultivates peace and stimulates interest and inspiration. This is the type of confusion that leads people to develop depression and mid-life crises, irrespective of the material abundance they have created for themselves.

Author Gary Zukov said that true peace comes about only when one's personality serves the purpose of one's soul. The 'why' we discover for ourselves is the only attribute we have that nothing and no one can take away from us. Therefore, financial abundance and society's version of success is not always relevant to a truly fulfilling life.

It is important to note that the reasons that drive us may change throughout our life. The intention to establish freedom by engaging in what we love to do may give way to becoming a dedicated parent and an example to our children. To know the 'why' behind our actions at any given stage of our life is to reveal the true source of what drives us. Once we know this, life becomes easier to structure and the things that are not relevant fall away almost automatically.

In light of this, I challenge us all to find out our "why" for the things we dedicate our time to as well as the things we are striving and working towards. Once we have written our list, let's ask us ourselves: are we living our life purposefully in the endeavours we have chosen for ourselves? If not, what can we do to accommodate that which truly aligns with the person we have become and find meaning in our life?

SECTION 2:
TAKING THE LEAP

DON'T TRY TO FIGURE IT ALL OUT

Have you ever driven a car at night during a wild weather storm? If you have, you know that you have to hyperfocus on the little bit you see in front of you to stay on the road. While you may maintain a mental vision of your destination, you only have access to a couple of meters in front of you at any one time. This analogy may seem random, but this is our life. Because we do not have a bird's eye view of how circumstances may unfold, we must make do by taking one small step at a time.

Let us think about the things that are worrying us at this very moment. It is most likely one of two things: something from the past, or uncertainty about our near or distant future. As the spiritual and thought leader Eckart Tolle points out, both are an illusion. What is real is only the moment in which we find ourselves, for by the time we get to the future we're anticipating, we will only ever be greeted with the present moment. Like the person driving the car in the heavy rain, whilst it is useful to have a vision of where we would like to get to, we only have access to the very next step we are about to take.

If we want to live a fulfilling and free life, we must accept this analogy and embrace it fully. Rejoice and find magic in this mystery that is our life and seek joy in every moment while taking baby steps towards that which feels like the next best thing. This attitude cultivates openness, faith, and most importantly, allows us to be present to the opportunities and green lights that are lighting up in front of us, which we might otherwise be missing.

Staying true and open means we can know the extent of the possibilities open to us, as when we fixate on a certain final destination, we may not realise that there is something even better suited out there for us.

I once knew a man whose dream was to become a stand-up comedian. Let's call him Adam. While on his journey, Adam randomly fell into a job as a home auctioneer. Within only a couple of years, he became one of the city's most sought-after auctioneers and started his own business, which is now hugely successful. He also offers training services to his peers in the industry. He got his wish to perform every day and uses his love for comedy to help people sell their homes. Watching him do his thing, it is obvious this role is meant for him. My point here is this: had Adam been closed off to other possibilities and insisted that stand-up comedy was his only path to fulfilment, he very easily could have missed this opportunity that has brought about abundance in so many areas of his life. We do not always know what the optimal outcome is or how what we seek will make its way to us. Sometimes, amid seeking something else altogether, we stumble upon that which is truly suited to our essence.

Staying open and paying close attention to the interruptions in our path will ensure we recognise that which is seeking us – even if it is not in the exact form we expect it.

The alternative to being present to each day is the agonising feeling of trying to figure everything out and therefore being a slave to the future. This is the reason many of us never take the leap towards that which makes our hearts sing. The how, where, when and who chatter is so overwhelming that it stops us in our tracks and puts the fire in our souls right out. The big lesson to take from Adam's journey is the importance of leaping in our quest for what we *think* may be best for us. No one took his goal to become a stand-up comedian seriously, but by remaining open and focused on his next step, he got to a place where he found his calling. How many of us are bold enough to go for that thing that might sound crazy to those around us?

THE TIME IS NOW

The possibility of being able to express my gifts and become financially free in the process always appealed to me. However, as is likely the case with many people, I was never presented with the perfect moment to get started. Instead, I had to create this perfect moment.

Before finally embarking on this journey with you all and sitting my bum down to add words to paper (or in this case my MacBook air) I had this sense that I needed to get to a particular stage where I was "sorted' or "found" in order to share the wisdom I had acquired. Never mind that I'm not sure what sorted even means. It was more a feeling that what I had learned so far was only part of the story and was not yet significant enough to share.

By the time I had the inspiration to start writing, I had already spent five years reading books, watching videos, and listening to podcasts on the topic of self-actualisation. But the most relevant part which I was missing was this: I, myself, had lived a lot of life and experienced its many nuances. When I realised what was holding me back, I saw how redundant it was. I had been caught up this whole time in the Disney-like narrative where my story would have a challenging start, a turbulent middle, and finally a destination in the form of a happily ever after where I was finally "found". It might seem ridiculous, but I challenge us all to ask ourselves how much of our life we've been living with this as the founding belief. I will do this when... – you fill in the blank.

What is true is that as constantly evolving beings, with change being the only constant and therefore the very premise of our existence, we will never be found, nor will we ever reach that dream destination because as soon as we do, there will be more to want. We can never put the book down to stop learning because life will never stop teaching. Once we make peace with this, it becomes easier to breathe. Instead, life really is about the delicious fruits we pick along the way and less about the buffet so many of us are desperate to get to. Here is where you get my full blessing (for whatever it's worth) to chill out and focus on enjoying the ride.

Out of the eight billion people here on earth, each one of us comes with a unique perspective and gift. Think about that mind-blowing fact; not one other person on earth has your unique colourful viewpoint of this life. Those who have acquired fulfilment and financial and spiritual freedom have capitalised on their unique point of view, be it through their creativity or their innovation. They did not wait to be experienced enough, old enough, educated enough or loved enough to do it.

I once listened to a podcast with an American finance guru who has helped thousands of people get out of debt. As she recounted her story, I was shocked that whilst she was charging hundreds of dollars for her services, she was in an astounding amount of debt herself. Similarly, some of the greatest artists and musicians of our time who have created timeless masterpieces were going through a low in their life. One does not need to be living out in the space of their desired destination to share a valuable perspective. So here I am sharing mine with you whilst not yet feeling entirely established in the sincere hope that it will prompt you to do the same.

I want us, dear readers, to get reflective about how our unique perspective can contribute to the world. Remember, there is not a single soul in the world that has walked in your shoes or faced challenges that are quite the same as yours. There is immense value in your perspective right now, so do not wait to start sharing it through your art, words, wisdom, or whatever way pleases you most.

GETTING STARTED

While we may not have it all figured out, it is important to make the first step toward the direction we think we may want to go. The great motivational speaker Lisa Nichols said it best: "I would rather you take ten wrong steps than none at all."

Whatever your ultimate vision for a fulfilling life is, the first step towards manifesting this change cannot be overemphasised. Irrespective of how insignificant it may seem, this small step serves a much bigger function in shifting our perception from what *is* to what *could* be. It increases our level of trust and communicates to the universe that we are ready and heading confidently towards that which we want. The minute this happens, we start to attract or recognise opportunities in our environment that will help us to get to where we are going.

Whether you are a believer in the law of attraction or simply view these phenomena from the perspective of confirmation bias, it is undeniable that once we reshape and sharpen our focus towards that which we seek, we become aware of elements in our environment (which we did not notice before) that contribute to and fit into this new vision. Bestselling author of *Mind Hack* David Bayer talks about the fact that we only take notice of twenty percent of what is going on around us. This twenty percent we zoom in on is shaped predominantly by our beliefs and chosen focus. When we shift our beliefs to what is possible, we open space to notice what is relevant outside our usual filtered focus.

My first step in writing this book was taking note of a series of observations about my life and the life of those closest to me. In the grand scheme of things, this step is minuscule. However, this small initiative did absolute wonders to cultivate an inspired state of mind. Taking this step every day to record my observations on paper caused me to start visualising myself in the role of an author and bring together the whole picture in my mind. What was more, I realised I already had all the tools and people I needed around me. Some were close friends and others were acquaintances, but each one of them was an expert in the exact area which I needed to realise my vision. What was interesting to me was that these people had been there all along. The only missing piece was my decision to make a move towards my vision. Taking this small first step worked miracles to open my awareness to all the assistance I already had around me.

> "When you want something, all the universe conspires in helping you to achieve it" – Paulo Coelho

Now is the time, dear reader, to take one small (or big) step towards that wonderful vision you've been putting on hold and to see how the universe swoops in to help by opening your awareness to the assistance you may presently be missing. What is the first step you will take?

COMMUNICATE YOUR STANDARDS; HAVE THE FAITH TO SAY NO

The law of attraction is about focusing thought on that which we desire to bring more of it into our lives. I want to take this concept one step further and talk about demonstrating what we want to the universe by saying *NO* to the things that are not serving us in our quest.

We set our standards through action; once our standards are demonstrated, life has no choice but to meet us where we have now placed ourselves. You will find many people, likely including you, and most certainly including myself, repeating patterns. This happens because we do not communicate our standards by saying no to what *is*. The saying "you get what you tolerate" is profoundly true.

A close friend was in the pattern of dating men who came on very strongly in the beginning but then failed to commit to a relationship. Finally, she broke up with someone she was starting to like because he did not know what he wanted from the relationship. This was the first time she had acted out so boldly and took a stand for what she wanted for herself. She felt sad about it but at peace that she had in this way communicated what she wanted – by saying no to that which she did not want. Not surprisingly, she met her partner, who she is still with today, only a couple of months later, following years of the same repeating pattern.

This idea can be applied to any area of our life. Another common example is a job, which we do not enjoy but have no plan of leaving because it pays well. Actor turned motivational speaker Kyle Cease gives a useful tool in deciphering between what is currently serving us and what we should say no to or let go of. He says that if we find ourselves often justifying a relationship or an experience in our mind, then it's a safe assumption that it should not be in our lives. When our actions are driven predominantly by that true and pure part of us, then the mind does not need to swoop in to justify the action. For example, we do not justify loving our friends and family members. This feeling and drive to be good to them just *is.*

Let us take a moment to think about all the experiences and relationships we are justifying to ourselves. It is worth noting the difference between *honestly acknowledging* a bad situation as such, but staying temporarily because it presently serves as a stepping stone to an improved circumstance, and *justifying* a bad situation by convincing ourselves it's the best we can do. In our list below, let us focus only on the later example, where we may be justifying a bad situation with no intention to make an improvement.

Having completed the above exercise and looking at our list, one might argue that justifications for these experiences stem from a need for security and stability. We hold onto things that are not for us in order to stay safe. Unfortunately, the need for safety is the primary reason that only a handful of us will ever be fulfilled in any area of our life. To communicate to the universe what we want, we must be brave enough to say goodbye to what we do not. It seems like a simple enough concept, but the reality is that letting go of what is familiar and known can be one of the scariest and most painful transitions we make, which is exactly why most of us never go through with it. The late poet Maya Angelou said "courage is the highest of all virtues" and I would add that in no circumstance is this truer than in the journey to self-actualisation. There is simply no value in knowing what is right for us if we do not dare to pursue it.

At least in my experience, being vocal enough about what I do not want has been perhaps the most challenging step of all, particularly in personal relationships. The trick, as I was so wisely told by my close friend, is to start small. Practice saying no to less significant things so that you are better practiced when it comes time to say no to the big things. As my biggest challenge, I am still working on this one, but based on my friend's experience and some of my own, I have full faith in the process and hope to master it (or come close to it) soon.

A recent example from my own life which demonstrates this principle is my decision to say no to the renewal of my contract for my desk job at a reputable London university. While I could not pinpoint anything particularly bad about my time there, it simply felt wrong. So, I turned this job down even though I had no idea where my income to pay the rent was going to come from. Luckily, I had some savings to get me through the next few weeks.

Instead of worrying about it during that time, I decided to enjoy my time and trust that it would all work itself out. I knew that I would sooner give up my dream of staying in London than say yes to another desk job. One beautiful sunny day, I was wandering around East London with a close friend, when I had the impulse to have a look at a coat stall. A man around my age greeted me and as we chatted about what size coat I needed, he mentioned that they needed someone to work part-time. Since this was one of my favourite destinations in London, without hesitation, I told him I was interested and ended up getting the job. The three months I spent working outdoors selling coats revived my soul and renewed my zest for life. It wasn't the job I wanted, but I got my wish to spend every day outdoors in the fresh air. I met creative people and artists who worked at the other stalls and with whom I shared many stimulating conversations. I used the time to reflect, get inspired again, and come up with new ideas and ways of moving forward. These days, whenever I feel doubtful about saying no to an opportunity that offers security only, I think back to this example and remember how (as long as I remain true to my highest aspirations) things will work themselves out.

Let us now start to take baby steps to demonstrate our standards to the universe by actively saying no to all that is no longer part of the vision we hope to realise. Visualise a stop sign when these people or things appear in our life. What are the things or people we find it difficult to say no to but know in our hearts we ought to? Let us make a list, then choose the easiest one to say no to today or the next time the opportunity arises.

DISCOVERING YOUR OWN PERSONAL BEST

The ability to say no to the things that do not align with who I am has been just as important, if not more important, than the things I have said yes to. In a sense, this means not settling for less than we know we can have.

To look deeply into ourselves and explore our personal best is to remove all the noise we are surrounded by and to enter a competition with only ourselves. While it is wonderful to appreciate the success others have achieved, the act of comparing our own journey to that of others is useless and detrimental. It is a bit like trying to win a race where all the opponents are taking a separate route to get to an entirely different destination. It seems absurd, and yet most of us spend too much energy taking score of where we are in this race with our peers.

Now that we have mentally kicked everyone out of the competition and have only ourselves to race against, let us take inventory of where we may be settling in our life. The most important part of this exercise is to remember that no one else can tell you what else might be possible for you. People around you may praise where you are in life, but you know deep down that this is not your best. Just because our life seems idyllic to the person across to you, that does not mean this is your own best. You may look like you have the perfect career and the perfect relationship to your friend, so you should be content and settle, but you know you can do better.

The feeling that we are being all that we can be is something deeply personal, so let us be as honest as we can in this exercise.

GIVING UP THE MYTH OF SECURITY

Our collective pursuit of security has always confused me. It occurred to me at a very young age that our lives have a final chapter and therefore the idea of feeling secure had to be an illusion – after all, how secure can we possibly feel knowing that we are all going to die sooner or later? My intent for highlighting this obvious truth is not to depress you, but instead to ask you to consider letting yourself off the hook when it comes to pursuing a sense of security.

Our tendency to sacrifice years of our life doing that which does not feel right or soul-serving to feel secure may be the single biggest obstacle to our progression as a species. Working a mediocre job to pay off a home and get a decent pension; marrying the partner that looks great on paper; buying the home that costs us the glorious experience of decades of freedom to roam and explore the world; chasing the career that promises *only* financial security – while there is nothing wrong with the aspirations I listed above, it is important not to mistake these for the security that keeps us from living a life that is impassioned and on purpose.

Remember, the house you think you own will only be yours for a few decades. The "great on paper" partner you married might have a change of heart and leave you to pursue his or her dream. There is no such thing as security in this life.

Instead, let us consider this: what if there exists a divine order operating on our behalf, and all that is required is to follow our peace and have faith in the bigger picture? What would life look like if we saw security as the illusionary concept that it is? What if we could adopt the perspective that our true security (this divine order) is already a given?

If you ask me, I still want it all: the beautiful London townhouse, maybe even a boat. But I want these to come as a by-product of living life on my own terms and in my own time, *not* as material objects I traded in for my soul so I can hide behind them and pretend I've made all that I can out of my life.

LONELY ON THE LEADING EDGE

At a certain point during my desperate attempt to find a blueprint for my life, I came to realise that there may not be one. As humans, we have a primal need to belong to a tribe and it is a natural impulse to look for an example, a standard, a framework to follow that has been formulated by someone somewhere to help validate our journey.

What we do not often think to imagine is that we may be in this alone, because *we* are the ones who are supposed to set the standard and pave a new way forward. This is where the phrase "it is lonely on the leading edge" came to me. Setting a brand-new way forward, whether in business, life, or both, can be incredibly exciting but at the same time scary, destabilising and lonely. We have been cradled by the norms of society, family and community for so long that deciding to do things differently feels unnatural to the conditioned part of our being.

What we need to remember is that most people who have contributed to humankind in a significant way have been alone on this journey and have had to pave the way for the rest of us with their own two hands. If you ever find yourself feeling lonely on your journey and feeling like most people in your life cannot relate to what you are trying to create, it can often mean that you're doing something right, not wrong. To face uncertainty on your journey and embrace it as a part of the wild ride that is life is to fully acknowledge and further embrace your role in being the creator you have been designed to be.

'My mind is a centre of divine operation. The divine operation is always for expansion and fuller expression, and this means the production of something beyond what has gone before, something entirely new, not included in past experience, though proceeding out of past experience by an orderly sequence of growth. Therefore, since the divine cannot change its inherent nature, it must operate in the same manner in me. Consequently, in my own special world in which I am the centre, it will move forward to produce new conditions always in advance of any that has gone before.'
–*Thomas Toward*

CREATING A BRIDGE BETWEEN THE PRESENT AND THE ASPIRATION

Becoming free is a process. Even though we were born free, our social conditioning is constantly pushing us not to stay this way. While I don't believe becoming free has to be difficult, one does need to maintain a consistent focus. One of the most important elements of this focus is the ability to visualise and re-enact who you wish to become and where you are wanting to go.

Because our actions are influenced by previous programming and conditioning, it is easy to forget where we are going. In my own experience, I have found that a daily reminder of where I wish to go and who I wish to become is the foundation for ensuring the small choices I make that day are contributing towards this vision. The power of this priming practice is to make our state of mind become less resistant to the newly imposed habits we want to adopt on our new journey.

An example of this practice is to think about what the person you aspire to be in your vision would be doing. How would their day be structured? Who would they surround themselves with? What kind of food would they be eating? What is the aesthetic that would surround them? Would it be nature? Beautiful architecture? How would this person dress and carry themselves?

Irrespective of whether our vision has come to life, acting as the person who is already enjoying this new way of being grounds and commits us to the vision, mind, body and soul. Whilst our life may not look exactly like the one we dream of, if we look, we can find aspects of it already in our everyday life.

What is most important is to approach this next exercise playfully and with an open heart and mind. If we do so, this is a surprisingly fun practice. For example, my current employer allows that I work remotely so that I do not have to be stuck in the office all day. In between being sat at a desk, I attend events so that my day is broken up. Whilst this is not my ideal job, I have taken what I *do* have and made from it the closest blueprint to the life I dream of. Instead of going into the office to work, I go to my favourite café, which requires me to ride through my favourite park where I pass the most beautiful houses. Whilst riding my bike, I listen to my favourite classical music, which calms my mind and brings about a feeling of peace and joy. I have always dreamt of working for people who inspire me. To an extent, this is something I have found in this new job too, so it is also something I like to focus on that has already been realised.

All these elements combined make me feel like I'm already living the life I dream of. This in turn means that the urgency and worry around achieving my goals dissipate, which brings about greater productivity and inspiration to do my best work.

Since being woken up by an alarm has borderline become a traumatic experience, I now go to sleep early enough that I will wake up when my body feels ready to and not have to be forced awake. Little actions like these make me feel abundant and in control. What matters is how our life looks to us, not how others perceive it. When applied with intention, our imagination is a powerful tool that allows us to make magic out of the mundane.

Remember, a miserable, half-hearted journey cannot lead to a fulfilling journey. If we are unable to single out and take pleasure in the circumstances we find ourselves in today, we will not know how to enjoy and appreciate any new improved conditions we create in the future. The trick is to already be there mentally to create more of that which we desire.

With this idea as our premise, let us take this opportunity to reflect on how our current life already resembles the one we are trying to create. What qualities about it are we already enjoying?

SECTION 3: BUILDING SELF WORTH

CULTIVATE A PLACE IN YOUR MIND THAT IS YOURS ONLY AND KEEP IT PRISTINE

From my own experience, talking to many of my peers and listening to hundreds of success stories, I have concluded that meditation, while highly effective, may not be for everyone. Instead, I believe we each have our own version of activities that help us to get back into the flow, and therefore can be just as effective as meditation.

A habit I developed as a child, which I have fondly carried on into adulthood, is taking time out every day to do something that brings peace and a feeling of centredness. These activities include reading, photography, dancing, listening to music, going for long walks and cycling. What is significant is that over the last twenty years I rarely recall missing days where I did not take at least an hour out for myself to engage in one or more of these. I remember a period when I had neglected to nurture this connection and it was a turbulent time in my life, if not the most turbulent.

My friends and family have always been familiar with my rituals and know to give me the time and space for them. These activities not only served to recharge, but to create a bond with myself that is unbreakable, unshakeable and built on loyalty. It doesn't matter what happens in my life, I always have this comfort and magic that I have created to go to, for me, by me. In this place, my imagination can flow freely and create a reality where I have the luxury to feel good, even if everything around me is falling apart.

This magic place I had cultivated made it easy for me to move to different countries and start a life of my own. I had established a relationship with myself where I had the faith to get through anything without needing others to accommodate my needs. This practice developed a solid self-esteem and made me feel invincible.

Living in a time when the media is obsessed with pointing out our individual and collective shortcomings, it is necessary to build up a practice to undo this conditioning and create space for more constructive beliefs and visions. Giving ourselves the time and space to tune out of our current circumstances and imagine another way becomes our door to realising the life we are seeking.

Let us make space each day to actively engage in a practice that requires soft focus – enough to tune out the noise of our current situation, but gentle enough to be soothing. The only rule to this practice is that it must be done alone, so that this magic place is not dependent on anyone outside us. For those of us who are extremely busy, this could be ten minutes of singing your heart out in the shower.

Try this practice for thirty days and see if you do not feel one hundred percent more connected to your life and the amazing people in it.

Use the space below to write some of these activities that we can bring into our life.

SPEND A PROLONGED PERIOD ALONE

This practice follows on from the previous one and takes it a step further in asking us to take ourselves away for a week (or whatever timeframe is available) to be with ourselves. There is something life-changing and magical that happens when we realise that not only does being alone not scare us, but that it can bring joy and fulfilment. This not only profoundly changes the relationship with ourselves, but with our closest and dearest. Once we realise that we are peaceful alone, we will not try to restrict someone else's desire for space (at least without realising straight away) nor will we require them to be something to us that they are not to themselves.

There is a level of self-acceptance that comes with being alone for a prolonged period. We are forced to face and reflect on all that we have been stuffing down and finally come to terms with it. This gives us the greatest chance to create the clarity and peace that would be difficult to conjure up with life consistently pulling us in all directions. What's more is that when we become at one with ourselves, with all our flaws and mistakes, by default we become more accepting and loving towards those in our life. We appreciate those amazing qualities in our loved ones and find it much easier to accept those traits that we are not so fond of.

The idea of this practice is not to shut people out or to learn to survive on our own. Trying to do this would be pushing against our basic biology. As a social species, building intimacy and high-quality relationships may be the single most important ingredient to living a fulfilling life. Instead, I propose this practice to train ourselves to be able to better embrace ourselves so that we have even more to offer to those we love most.

KEEPING THE PROMISE

The path to freedom demands that we develop respect for ourselves and for our journey. Since there are no classes in school to teach us about developing self-respect, most of us, myself included, have had to learn the hard way. I have found the most basic way to cultivate self-respect is through discipline.

The irony of seeking freedom through disciplined action does not escape me. For a free spirit like myself, discipline may be my least favourite term in the English language. However, I can no longer deny that it has been a fundamental part of cultivating a peaceful and therefore productive state. The simple practice is this: do not break the promises you have made to yourself. Note that I did not include the word "try". To say that we will try is the surest way to set ourselves up for failure. So here it is again:

<u>Do not break the promises you have made to yourself.</u>

That's it. This may seem like an obvious hack, but it turns out hardly anyone does it consistently. It takes an elevated amount of focus to keep the standards we have for ourselves high, with life giving us so many tempting options. For example, you have planned to go for a run, but your friend has suggested you go out and see a movie. For once, you want to go for your run but feel torn about what to choose, as you also want to see your friend. In this scenario, choosing to go for your run will earn you self-respect. This action may seem insignificant in the grand scheme of things, but it becomes incredibly powerful to your self-esteem if kept up over time. After all, your life is the sum of all your moment-to-moment decisions over a prolonged period.

For me, the practice of keeping the promises I have made to myself proved a powerful way to build true self-worth and confidence. With life constantly happening to us, this may not always be possible due to circumstances bigger than ourselves, however, as I have found in my own experience, sticking to our word even eighty percent of the time will yield notable results. Conversely, consistently breaking our promises results in the opposite: the feeling that we are consistently betraying ourselves, which inevitably leads to low self-worth and a lack of trust in what we can achieve. If we find ourselves noticing that we have low self-confidence, it is worth exploring where in our lives we are constantly breaking promises to ourselves.

Use the space below to pinpoint where you have broken your word to yourself in the last month and take the opportunity to reflect on the reason for this and whether there is room to improve.

Now that we have had the opportunity to become aware of where we have been letting ourselves down, let us use the space below to make a single promise or list of promises to ourselves and apply this practice for thirty days. This does not have to be anything world-changing and could be as simple as meditating for twenty minutes each day.

To give you an idea of how simple this could be, here are the promises I have made to myself.

1. Start every day with tea and lemon juice

2. Meditate for 20 minutes

3. Do some light stretching

4. Ride my bicycle to work irrespective of the weather conditions

No matter what your list contains, consistency in this practice is key. Once we have proven to ourselves that we can stick to a self-betterment practice consistently, we build trust in our focus and ability, and in this way prepare for much bigger things. How we do anything is how we do everything. An unorganised room is often a reflection of an unorganised life. In other words, a lack of discipline in one area often shows up in all areas. I have by no means reached the version of me that I know is possible, but I am encouraged by the little steps I can stick to and continue adding to my list of promises. Remember, staying true to our word builds self-respect which may be the only thing we can do to free ourselves from the lack of self-worth most people spend their life tolerating.

Once you have identified your practice(s), write it/them down, date the statement and sign your piece of paper. Congratulations!

You have now entered a binary contract with yourself in the form of a promise. Disclaimer: it may be the most important promise(s) you ever keep.

DO NOT ASK PEOPLE FOR ADVICE ABOUT YOUR LIFE PATH

One thing that many successful people have in common is the ability to trust their own instinct and act on it. We all come with an extremely sophisticated, in-built guidance system in the form of the wild self, intuition, or deeper knowing – whatever we choose to call it. Everything we need to make any big or small decision about our life is already innate and accessible to us at all times.

By making clarity and peace in our state of mind the primary goal, we can confidently rely on the internal messages we get regarding what decision we should make and what path to take. If practiced well enough, we get to a place where we do not need to rely on the opinion of others to determine our next best step.

The importance of practicing and trusting our own guidance is primarily to ensure we stay true to ourselves. Further, it ensures we take full responsibility for our lives and take the lead in all decisions that affect our lives. This is not to suggest that an alternative perspective cannot help in evaluating our options. Every now and then we are not in tune with this clarity, get stuck in our own heads and need the right people to broaden our view. It is important, however, to ensure the decision we make is ultimately our own and that we have not delegated it to the person whose opinion we are seeking.

Each time we decide in accordance with someone else's opinion, we are giving away our power. Abandoning ourselves in this way also encourages others to do the same through our example. A mother who is making decisions according to what her family demands is a very common circumstance where this is the case. While the deed is beautiful, this behaviour can be destructive on two fronts: one, the mother is neglecting her own needs and cannot sustain giving to others if she is not taking care of herself; and two, as the role model for the children, she is teaching her daughter to delegate her own decision-making too in her future role as a mother.

The other piece to this is that people around us have their own perceptions and agenda for our life. A father who wants to protect his child may be unlikely to support them in their engagement with anything he deems risky, not out of spite but out of love. Irrespective of where it is coming from, it is important to stay true to our calling and vision. In my own experience, even the wrong decisions I made on my own were much easier to swallow than the ones I made following someone else's advice.

Let us reflect on the last big decision we made. Was this decision inspired from within, or influenced by someone close to us? The answer to this question may be a good indication of to what extent we trust and value our own judgment. Applying some or all the practices prescribed in this text will act to cultivate an increased level of trust and encourage us to take full responsibility for the decisions we make regarding our path.

THE ROLE OF FEAR

As I've discovered in my journey, fear of the unknown is the only factor holding us back. I thought it essential to dedicate a chapter to gaining a more liberating perspective on this roadblock. Through self-reflection and watching other people, I have concluded that our fear stems from our inability to tune out the consistent doubt-filled chatter in our heads. New Age thought leaders refer to this as the monkey brain.

To demonstrate my idea of the monkey brain, I use the term brain as separate and in contrast to spirit, soul, wild self - that which we truly are.

While our world has significantly evolved since the dark ages, our brain has not kept up with this trend. As cave people, it served us as a detector for threats in our environment. During that time, food was scarce and mere survival was an uphill battle. Today, for those of us fortunate enough to live in a peaceful part of the world, an immediate threat to our survival is not something we are challenged with daily, yet the brain is still programmed by default to be on the lookout for threats to try and protect us.

Consequently, once our brain finds a safety zone, it will be extremely resistant to novelty and change. It is enough to look around at the number of people in our life who are terrified to change their ways. Some spiritual teachers refer to this ancient mechanism as the ego, which is the part of us that is always on the defence for some reason or another, living out our life from a place of fear and scarcity. In practice, this might be the persistent belief that we are not good enough, that people are out to get us, and the world is a scary and dangerous place that does not support us. The brain does this to keep us safely locked up in our usual patterns.

These often unconscious fears are manifested in various ways, the most common being an obsessive drive for a feeling of security, stability, and generally staying in our corner while carefully avoiding anything that does not fit in with our worldview. While it is true that the fear most of us carry within us can be attributed to specific trauma we have experienced at some point in our life, it is important to know that just because it is justified does not mean it is constructive.

In the context of creating an extraordinary life for ourselves, the first thing to do is realise that our brain is a threat detector. It can be impulsive and paranoid at best and limiting and even destructive at its worst. To cultivate peace, this consistent chatter must be recognised as the paranoid friend rather than the decision-maker in our life. Due to our conditioning and biological wiring this not an easy pattern to break, but it can be done simply with regular practice. This is where some form of meditation can help. The practice of silencing this chatter allows us to connect with what is the truest and most real part of us, our spirit. Regular practice allows us to be led, more often, by our heart and intuition, the wild child, the magical part of us that cannot be explained nor contained.

So, my dear readers, unless we really are being chased by a lion or in some form of immediate danger, let us choose faith over fear next time it arises. This will not happen overnight, but with a regular meditation practice in place, in whatever form that works for you, we activate the parasympathetic nervous system and become less reactive to the threats we perceive around us. I leave you to think this over with the wise and true words of

Franklin Roosevelt who said “the only thing we have to fear is fear itself.”

Let us make a list of our greatest fears at this moment. It may be useful to dissect where each of these fears comes from and how it is poses a tangible threat to us or not. For example, the fear of public speaking does not pose a tangible physical threat, as opposed to a fear of losing our job which may leave us homeless and therefore is a more significant threat to our overall wellbeing.

Now that we know which fears we have that are intangible, what if we acknowledged their presence, but took the leap anyway?

WEEDING THE MIND

This next chapter explores further how we can turn the volume down on the voice of the monkey brain and increase the volume on the voice of our intuition or wild self.

Over the last decade, nutrition and physical wellbeing have become a central theme in people's lives. Every day, there is a new diet to try and a new way to become physically stronger and leaner. Most people aspire to have an optimal body. Our diet and exercise regime has become a mainstream conversation and an ever-expanding industry.

While there is no denying that looking after our physical well-being is essential, what is also important but less emphasised (until very recently) is the importance of maintaining our mental and emotional state. I would personally rate this as a higher priority as I have found that a balanced state of mind breeds a balanced way of living, and therefore an optimal physical state as a by product. To put it simply, a balanced, clear mind will be inspired to take healthy and balanced action.

Joe Dispenza's compelling research on epigenetics, commencing in his book *You Are the Placebo* and most recently *Becoming Superhuman,* is now supported by several ground-breaking thought leaders and new age physicians such as Deepak Chopra, Bruce Lipton, and many others. The research reveals the power of our thoughts to influence positive or negative changes in our bodies. Dr Dispenza talks about his first-hand experience of healing his critically injured back through consistent meditation and discipline of the mind. This discipline and faith resulted in him walking again shortly after being told he never would. What Dr Dispenza's research suggests is that the most powerful tool in creating our best possible life is the consistent maintenance of the mind.

I like to think of our mind as a garden; unless we take the time to get rid of the weeds, they will eventually start taking over. These weeds are made up of limiting beliefs, past conditioning, negative experiences, and most often trauma. They act as a set of programs that influence our actions and reactions, not based on what we want or need, but on what is already known to our experience. As Einstein so wisely pointed out, "the definition of insanity is doing the same thing over and over again and expecting different results." For this reason, unless we pay attention to how we are being controlled by our past conditioning, we will find it incredibly difficult to create anything new. An interesting question to ask ourselves each day is this: how free are we from ourselves?

A mediocre attitude to life requires minimum maintenance of the mind, and this is unfortunately where most people live. In my research for this text, there was not a single highly fulfilled person that did not engage in a practice to keep their mind in line every single day. Many supplemented this practice with physical exercise, but the main goal is always to centre oneself and to create mental and emotional clarity relating to who they truly were and where they wish to go.

A free and extraordinary life, therefore, demands that we give the same time and attention to our minds as we do to our bodies.

You will hopefully have noticed that all chapters so far have communicated a consistent aim: to cultivate an optimum state of mind in as many ways as possible. It is important to find out or to invent what works best for you and make it an everyday habit that becomes as essential as showering or brushing your teeth.

IF YOU WOULDN'T SAY IT TO A FRIEND, DO NOT SAY IT TO YOURSELF

A close friend was going through some common challenges in her relationship. As she was describing the situation, I noticed she often referred to herself in a self-deprecating way. She repeated that she could not control her emotions and as a result lashed out at her partner – it was all her fault, and she needed to get herself together. Her story, while likely partly true, was not the whole picture, yet this was the part she was focused on. As a result, she was not only depressed about the situation, but also furious at herself for her reaction to it.

This made me think back to the time when I was going through a similar circumstance, and how kind and patient she was in trying to soothe me. It begged the question why she was not showing herself the same compassion. The fact is that many of us would never talk to our friends the way we talk to ourselves. Recognising this destructive and mostly very unconscious habit is rooted in a deep feeling of unworthiness.

The first step to address this issue is to take note of the commentator in our head – that voice that mostly drives our actions and seems to have an opinion and hold a judgment about everything we do.

Let us become keenly aware from this moment of what kind of conversation we are having with ourselves. What kind of language are we using? What is the general tone of voice? Is it optimistic or critical? Is it demanding or soothing? Each time we catch ourselves criticising, let us dig deep and see if there is any foundation to these accusations. Once we become aware of what we are telling ourselves, it becomes possible to change this story.

The reality is that most of us take the way we relate to ourselves for granted and do not even notice the stories we tell ourselves. I hope that this exercise will bring to light our relationship with ourselves – after all, to become all that we can be, the first step we need to take is to become our own best friends.

NOTHING IS PERSONAL

We are all born into this world with our own preferences and perspectives. There are billions of worlds happening simultaneously – one world for each person. We all live in our funny little bubbles where we are the main character of our story.

Our perceptions are therefore little more than reflections of what is going on inside of us. The late author Wayne Dyer used the analogy that when you squeeze a lemon, you can only ever get lemon juice. What he was illustrating is that when we are put under pressure (just as a lemon when it is squeezed), it is what is inside us that will come out. If at our core we are frustrated, this is what will surface. If we love, even under pressure, this is what will come out. When a person acts out of line, it often reflects what is dwelling inside of them, and has little to do with us.

The famous student and teacher of *A Course in Miracles* Marianne Williamson suggests that when someone betrays us, the quickest way to get past this is to pray for this person. While this is counterintuitive, particularly in extreme cases of betrayal, we need to remind ourselves that the resentment we carry around for others is hurting us more than it is anybody else. The act of forgiving interrupts the negative momentum and releases us from the pain caused by the betrayal. It takes away the power to control our lives away from the other person.

This is not to say that we should ignore intense emotions and leave them unexpressed. The act of consistently pretending to be positive and ignoring one's emotions is extremely detrimental, both emotionally and physically. However, we can choose to express our anger and frustration in other ways that do not include holding on to bitterness towards the other person.

Intimate relationships hold up a mirror for what is going on deep down in the abandoned parts of ourselves. It is intimate relationships that give us the opportunity to learn most about forgiveness, self-acceptance and the acceptance of those we love. Precisely for this reason they are a central part of the human experience and our individual evolution. They simultaneously nurture, challenge, uplift and shake our beliefs in a way that nothing else can, and consequently bring us to a forever changed place. I believe many of us are desperately seeking out our soulmate because we are craving this evolution on a subconscious level.

Let us practice letting those who have disappointed us off the hook. Whether we choose to voice our opinion is less relevant – what matters are the internal conversations we are having about this person and the story and meaning we are attributing to their behaviour. Avoid assumptions and take back your power by giving those around you the benefit of the doubt.

> "Forgive others, not because they deserve forgiveness, but because you deserve peace" – Jonathan Lockwood Huie

WHAT ARE OUR STANDARDS FOR OUR LIFE AND WHERE DO THEY COME FROM?

We often get lost in other people's standards and take those up as our own. I like to refer to these as adopted standards. A simple way to ensure the standards we set out are truly our own is to list the reason for them. When we ask ourselves why we are striving for something, it helps pinpoint where this standard came from. For example, you may have grown up in a twelve-bedroom house and thus the standard is that you can house your own family in a twelve-bedroom house. This standard may be a form of subconscious conditioning and something we are driven by without even realising it.

Becoming aware of an adopted standard allows us to decide whether this is what we truly want. This practice is simple but has been remarkably effective at weeding out my own adopted standards. For example, I wanted so much for my parents to be proud of me that my first thought about taking any action was: "what would mum and dad say?" The idea that my parents would be pleased was often enough to constitute the go-ahead on an important decision. We all have an unquenchable desire to be loved and to belong, particularly by our parents or caregivers. This should not be ignored nor suppressed, but if the first answer for our question "why do I have this standard" is how happy it would make our parents or peers, it's time to dig deeper to ensure we are not betraying our own priorities.

Use the space below to list the standards we have set out for our life and let us reflect on each to ensure they are really ours.

SETTING THE STANDARDS BUT GIVING UP THE EXPECTATIONS

Now that we have a clearer idea on the standards we would like to carry forward for our lives, let us look at how we may apply these.

As mentioned earlier, one of the most liberating ideas we can adopt on our life journey is to embrace that the world does not owe us anything. This way of thinking allows us to control our state of being, without relying on the actions of others or the circumstances surrounding us to add or take away from our peace. This means giving up the expectation that life and the people in it should be different and that we should be in receipt of something.

Furthermore, it seems that only when we give up the expectation for something it becomes free to make its way to us. Have you ever noticed that the things you want lightly come easily, while the things you want badly take their time or never show up at all? When we spend our energy dwelling on something that has not come, we are wasting energy that could otherwise be focused elsewhere, and simultaneously creating the very block that is keeping it away. Often it is our full engagement in the joy of the process that will bring about results, not our pursuit of the outcome.

Keeping our expectations low allows us the luxury of peacefully detaching ourselves and walking away from people and things that do not align with our standards. It means accepting the situation for exactly what it is and skipping the drama of trying to change a person or circumstance, instead channelling this energy into something productive. Knowing when to walk away from situations that are not in harmony with my vision (and not feeling bad about it) may be the most useful skill I have gained in my adult life.

Whilst keeping our expectations low, we can keep our standards high. Keeping the standard high for our life and for ourselves is the only thing we are in control of; this is the beauty of making this our sole focus.

When it comes to standards for our personal relationships, the key is to communicate our desires *without the expectation that the other person will agree to fulfil them.* Our only responsibility is to take the (sometimes very challenging) step of communicating our standard. There is no regard for the outcome in this practice. Once our message is communicated, what the other person does with this information is not any of our business and not something we take responsibility for or try to control.

This practice of owning and communicating our standards to the world will ensure that eventually we will find the people and circumstances who are happy to meet us where we are.

Let us reflect on what area in our life we would like to raise the standard for and write it down. Next, pick at least one of these points and challenge yourself to take the step of communicating it.

APPLY HARD FOCUS

After watching hundreds of hours of interviews with entrepreneurs, thought leaders and athletes who have achieved remarkable success, I found that hard work was overstated as a top contributor to success. Many people work incredibly hard for decades and do not get very far from where they started. While hard work is often a component of success, it is not the driving factor.

This is key, as the idea of working hard may be what is keeping us from venturing down our desired path. In the following chapter, I hope to remove this assumption from our collective pile of excuses.

Upon closer inspection, I realised two significant things: one is that for most people with an extraordinary life, their work is a labour of love. It is the thing they would spend the rest of their days doing, even if it did not amount to financial success or influence change in the world. As someone who has many things I love to do, I can say with certainty that the hours spent doing things we love do not qualify as work, much less 'hard work', as people tend to refer to it.

Secondly, I noticed that where the individual did not necessarily love what they did, there was always a purpose bigger than their own life that they were pulled to serve. When a person has discovered a purpose and drive in this world, they cannot help but follow it. I list this as a separate point because I'm not entirely convinced that we all come here with a specific purpose. As Matt

Haig so eloquently put in his novel *Notes on a Nervous Planet*, "we are the purpose". Even without a clear theme or pursuit, we are enough just existing in the world. In this context, 'purpose' simply means trusting our intuition or wild self to lead us.

While writing off hard work as a top ingredient to fulfilment and success, what I did find all successful and abundant people have in common is a concept I call hard focus.

The idea of focusing on the vision may seem like an obvious contributor. However, achieving this level of resilience depends on several underlying beliefs and actions, the most important of which are:

1. A belief that what we are striving for will eventuate in some form.

2. The ability to trust the process, even when achieving the goal seems impossible.

3. The belief that we are worthy of the vision we seek.

4. Consistently and continually taking actions to make progress toward our vision, irrespective of how small.

5. Ensuring every decision we make, big or small, is in integrity with our vision.

6. The ability to align with the "why" of our vision.

With these practices and beliefs in place, there is no reason why our journey towards that which we seek needs to include extreme sacrifice and hard work.

SECTION 4: NURTURING AND STRENGTHENING THE WILD SELF – OUR INTUITION

TAKE A DAY OUT TO FOLLOW YOUR FEET

Dedicating time to develop and give a voice to our intuition, or our wild child, cannot be overemphasised. Whether we are pulled to serve humanity on a mass scale or are here to live an impassioned life and influence others to do the same through our example, we must be led by this mysterious part of us. The following is an exercise that will help to give the wild child space to operate on our behalf. This wild child is our intuition and the wisest part of us of all.

Take off the morning, afternoon, or a whole day, if possible, to be led purely by your intuition. This exercise requires no plans or aspirations. We are simply going to throw on our favourite attire and step out into the complete unknown and practice acting purely on impulse. Do I want to go right or left at the end of this street? Without any thought or justification, follow what comes to you first. What has been significant for me during this exercise is that each time I have done this has led me to discover something new about the surrounding area that I live in or even meet new people. It's as if our body knows things we have not yet attuned to and will take us to exactly the place we have been wanting to find ourselves.

Pay special attention to inspired actions or paths that go directly against our logic and rational mind. For example, let's say you are on a tight budget, but your impulse is to get a coffee at an expensive café. Provided the money you have is not going to be your last meal, have the faith to follow the impulse. Each time I have had a strong pull to do something, even though it made no sense at all to my rational mind and went ahead and did it, something magical happened to me. Either I have discovered an opportunity or met a person who inspired me in some way. This is also an excellent way to give our brains a rest from the mundane details of life.

Following this exercise makes us notice the space and freedom to play that is always available to us. Purely following our intuition helps us to trust ourselves in a deep way that is impossible to be questioned by the monkey brain. The wild child has finally been given permission to take over and wants you to know this: a person whose mind has been cultivated into a state of freedom will have no limits.

TAKE YOURSELF OUT OF YOUR ROUTINE AT LEAST ONCE A DAY

In acknowledgment that some of us are incredibly busy and may not have the luxury to take hours out of the day to follow our feet as suggested in the previous chapter, here is a less time-consuming way to strengthen our relationship with our intuition and wild self.

What I propose is to take ourselves out of our routine at least once a day.

Wherever you find yourselves dear readers, this practice could look like taking a new route to work, getting coffee from a different place than usual, or going for a wander instead of eating at the desk during lunch hour. When we make it a conscious choice to keep learning and expanding the box we are in, life does not have the chance to become stale and meaningless. Our perspective begins to broaden as does the space to hear our intuition.

Let us add "permitting ourselves to expand every day" to the list of promises we make to ourselves. What could we do differently this week that might create a shift in our perspective and broaden it just a little?

ACTIVELY SEEK TO CULTIVATE THE FLOW STATE

We all long to lose our minds every now and then. It is what is behind every one of our vices. We seek an opportunity to feel the wholeness and the totality of who we are.

Art in any form is the channel to this transcendence. It is the back door that in an instant, bypasses our rational mind and gives us the potential to reach a mental state of expansion and freedom. For a lot of people, myself included, it is music that most powerfully and easily provides this channel to an altered state of being. Knowing the type of music that elevates us and takes us out of our monkey brain is an incredibly effective tool that can be used to uncover our deepest-rooted desires. It stimulates the visceral in us; what cannot be explained, only felt. The more we can encourage this feeling, the better in touch with our true selves we become. All actions that will assist us to become our liberated selves are inspired from this truthful place.

In our quest for a life that is beyond our wildest dreams, I encourage us all to spend time reflecting on what type of music sends us into an altered state and makes us feel elevated and alive. It is also worth pointing out that some music, while wonderful, may influence a build-up of heavy emotion and therefore lack full thinking. It Is best, in my own experience, to focus on music that inspires in us the feeling of heightened positive energy, light-heartedness, playfulness, aliveness, expansiveness, calmness and invincibility.

Once we have established what type of music makes us feel this way, we can go ahead and put together a playlist that can accompany us throughout our day. The effects of uplifting music on our mood can be remarkably healing and elevating. In my own experience, music has a way of transporting me into a different reality by shifting my perspective to such a degree that I forget who I am and completely get lost in it. This is when we become acutely attuned to the wild child and to the field where all things are possible.

Use the space below to write a list of songs that make you feel joyful, alive and inspired and begin to put together your most important playlist.

BE FULLY PREPARED FOR THE BEST POSSIBLE SCENARIO

An important lesson I learned has been that when I envision a desire, I better be prepared to receive that which I have asked for. There were many incidences where I failed this very simple principle. I would ask for something but would not create the space in my mind to have it become a reality. When this event, person or experience then did manifest, I was unprepared and ran away from the situation or sabotaged it without meaning to.

This lack of preparation is the feeling of not being worthy of that which we are seeking. Oprah Winfrey wisely said that destiny is opportunity meeting readiness. Unfortunately, experience teaches better than words, so I only now have a true appreciation of what Oprah meant by the term 'readiness'.

My latest example of this is a funny story where I found myself face to face with a very famous actor. It was a sunny day, and I quite literally took a page out of my own book and decided to follow my feet for the day. No aspirations and no plans – just the way I described it in the previous chapter. Suddenly, I saw a tall figure walking in front of me and heading into the vintage markets. Weirdly, I knew from his back that he was significant in some way. I had yet to walk past the vintage markets and not peek at the perfectly tailored sixties designer pieces on offer, but today I was less interested and was led by the mystery man.

The next thing I knew, I looked around me and found myself one of ten or so women huddled around the clothes stand. It seemed that I was the only one in the pact that was not entirely sure of what the commotion was about, even though I suspected this tall man was the centre of it. Feeling uncomfortable being in a pack of swooning women I walked in the other direction and silently voiced to the universe that if I was meant to speak to this man, he would come and find me.

I left in the opposite direction and within minutes was contemplating trying on a white nineties t-shirt having forgotten all about the mystery man. Suddenly I looked up and there he was. Also looking at the same shirts and straight at me. This was when I finally caught on – he was a very famous actor from the series everyone had been talking about. I had fantasised about this very moment many times before and admittedly someone very similar to him is the centre of this vision.

Yet instead of smiling back at him, I turned on my heels and walked away. Why? Because I did not feel worthy or prepared for this fantasy to be realised. There was nothing logical about my behaviour, but there it was.

We have all experienced unusual situations which often seem to come out of nowhere and catch us off guard. Running into that person, being offered a career-related opportunity at very short notice, and many other big or small experiences we did not show up for in the way we intended. The question is then: how do we prepare for what we have asked for? The solution I have since adopted is to imagine the best thing that could happen to me every time I leave the house.

We spend most of our life preparing for the worst-case scenarios by purchasing overpriced insurance packages and perusing a life of security. What if we were to use this energy to prepare for the best possible experience instead?

Let us come up with our best-case scenario of something that could happen to us each day and rehearse this before we leave our home to go out into the world. We could also take it a step further by dressing for the occasion and acting as though it is just about to happen. This is the time to be outrageous and reach for the stars. Disclaimer, be careful what you wish for because you WILL get it.

KEEP OUR IDENTITY FLUID

> "Be like water making its way through cracks. Do not be assertive, but adjust to the object, and you shall find a way around or through it. If nothing within you stays rigid, outward things will disclose themselves. Empty your mind, be formless, shapeless, like water." – Bruce Lee

This is just one of the many quotes where Martial Arts master Bruce Lee emphasises the importance of remaining fluid. This one is my favourite as it most clearly articulates a profound truth about our identity and spirit. Keeping our identity fluid means seeing ourselves as forever evolving and adapting beings. For example, we may have one personality at work, another one in a social setting, and be entirely someone different with our intimate partner. It appears that one person is playing out multiple personalities, but the reality is that as spirits, we have multiple personalities, and to cling to one is to deny and suppress the other versions of ourselves which are just as authentic.

Our personalities can be looked at like an outfit we wear to an event. Whether the event is a wedding or a business conference will determine what we choose to wear. But at the heart of it, this outfit is still a version of our unique essence because we still get to choose what it will be.

Keeping our personality fluid means being open to the diversity and contrast of life, and most importantly our evolution as well as the evolution of others. After all, change is the only true constant we can rely on. Avoiding identifying ourselves with what is external is at the heart of this philosophy.

Someone might identify with a certain political view so strongly that changing this label would threaten who they perceive themselves to be. The typical trap we fall into is identifying ourselves by our career, our possessions and even by our relationships. A mother, for example, may lose sight of who she was before being a carer for her children. While there is nothing wrong with embracing the role of motherhood fully, it may become an obstacle when this role is no longer required in the same way. She might, for example, fall into a depressive state when her children move out if she has not learned to nurture other parts of herself and recognise that she is an evolving being. Others will identify themselves with their wealth and let their possessions own them instead of the other way around. What is more, this attitude of labelling ourselves in certain ways prevents us from being open to people and experiences that may not fall into the same group, and therefore shuts us away in a little bubble.

So what is the validity of Bruce Lee's philosophy in our practical day to day lives? Here is how I apply this principle: Author and leader in peak performance Todd Herman asks his clients to identify and embody an alter ego that will assist them in achieving their goals. The process involves the client choosing an archetype who is successful in a particular area, and then to adopt or activate their exact attributes. A notable example of how powerful this technique can be is the alter ego created by artist and singer Beyonce to assist her confidence when performing on stage. When Beyonce steps on stage, she leaves behind her adolescent history as a modest gospel singer and becomes a provocative, powerful performer as her alter ego, who she named Sasha Fierce.

Let us explore our personalities. Who are we at work, and who are we with our loved ones? Is there a part of ourselves we can activate to help us become a better version of ourselves in these areas? Can creating an alter ego that matches our ideal help us to become this new and improved version?

To identify an alter ego for ourselves, it is useful to go back to the section about discovering our essence. Identifying people we admire and unpacking the specific qualities we admire about them can give us clues for which of these we would like to embody. As children, roleplaying and changing identity was natural as breathing. Let us adapt that playfulness and see how it benefits us to step into the shoes of the person we admire the most to serve us in a particular situation.

SECTION 5: GETTING READY TO BE READY

REFRAIN FROM TRYING TO FIGURE OUT WHY THINGS FEEL WRONG OR WHY THEY DID NOT WORK IN THE PAST

One of my tendencies while navigating my way through life was to spend too much energy trying to figure out why certain parts did not work out. After what turned out to be years of trying to get to the bottom of why my most significant romantic relationship to date had not worked out, I realised there was no bottom. While there was unquestionable value in reflecting on what the relationship had taught me and who I had been in it, I had spent too much time holding on to what had happened.

For the longest time, I blamed him, then myself, shifting my resentment back and forth in a desperate attempt to learn what the objective truth about us was – only to realise that there is no such thing, and there would never be a satisfying enough conclusion to our story.

The beauty I was missing was that I was free to make whatever I wanted out of it and there was little value in picking apart the timeline to see if I had missed something. Author Caroline Mace says "if you try on a dress and it does not fit, you do not sit there questioning why this is or wondering how you could make it fit. Instead, you simply move on and try another one." While leaving a person or a life circumstance is inevitably an emotionally turbulent experience, it is important to keep life simple and draw the line for ourselves somewhere to ensure we do not become slaves to past experiences.

Let us explore in what ways we remain enslaved by our past. What about these situations are we in resistance about? Once we find out the answer to this, we can begin to accept this situation and to choose something else to focus on. In doing this, we'll be able to leave behind that which is now water under the bridge.

While I appreciate this is something that is much easier said than done, there is a technique that has worked for me every time: to sit with my pain, without looking for distractions. While this exercise may be uncomfortable and counterintuitive, something amazing happens every time. The longer I sit with the feeling, the less of a grip it has on me. I am not a psychologist, but I imagine that this is similar to how exposure therapy works.

By letting myself feel as bad as I can, I give up the struggle and let go of the need to control. Eventually, something strange and unexpected happens – I get bored of myself being in this state and slowly the joy starts to creep back into my being. The more we face our feelings and release them, the less power they have over us and therefore the freer we become.

Let us take the opportunity to write down everything in our life we are holding on to. Once we know what this is, let us take some time out to face the pain head on and see what happens.

KNOW THAT YOU'RE ALREADY A SUCCESS

Looking at our life from a place of abundance is paramount to cultivating a peaceful state, from which all good things will flow. This may be the most important part of this text. If you take nothing else away, remember this: you are already a success. Do not buy into the standards pushed on us by society about what this means. We live in a world where a human is valued by their financial worth. While this is a fantastic by-product, on its own it has little to do with what is true to us or healthy, and yet we all get caught up in playing the game – which is perfectly fine, so long as we recognise it as such. This is not to say that we should not appreciate the finer things in life. There is no denying it is beautiful to enjoy the material comforts, but it is equally important not to mistake these for the final destination or a part of our identity. Instead, we recognise that what we have been entrusted with at this very moment is nothing short of a miracle.

Start to practice appreciation every day until it becomes automatic and the dominating attitude we have towards our life. This shift happens gradually but is an incredibly significant and powerful one. It is only from this place of abundance that our paths will open and lead us to the freedom we have been seeking. When we realise that we are already a success, it takes away the stress and urgency to acquire it and we start to enjoy our journey towards that which we want.

Remember, a successful and joyful life is nothing more than

creating beautiful moments which amount to minutes, which amount to hours, days, months, and years.

“There are only two ways to live your life: as though nothing is a miracle, or as though everything is a miracle” – Albert Einstein.

Let us make it a weekly practice to list all the miracles in our life. What made us smile today? How have we made the most of our day? Who are the people that lit up our world that little bit, and in what ways is life serving us at this very moment?

Use the space below to write a list of ten things that you are grateful for today.

CHANGE IS THE NECESSARY CONSTANT

American author Esther Hicks says that to be at peace, we must keep up with who we have become. As human beings, we are constantly evolving. Each experience gives rise to a new desire or preference. The discord between who have been and who we have become causes us psychological and physical pain. I have discovered some of my most significant growth through painful experiences because I ignored the signs that it was time to move on.

This is the reason there is so much emphasis on staying true to oneself throughout this text. Self-development author and spiritual teacher Michael Beckwith claims that we must consistently be evolving and reaching for more, in whatever individuated way that looks like for each of us. The consequence of standing still provokes life to push us towards evolution, which is often through pain and a direct result of ignoring what we know at our very core.

Let us reflect on our lives and the events that brought us to where we are. Often, we find ourselves heading down the wrong path but are too afraid to turn back. It is for this reason that it is so important to become in tune with who we are so that we become more efficient at recognising when to move on from a present situation which no longer serves us. The process of becoming in tune with our intuition and the courage to pursue what we know is right paves the way to evolve *joyfully* instead of a *painful*ly. But evolve we must either way.

This practice will not eliminate the challenges life has for us, but since evolution is the only constant, I hope it will prompt us to be accepting and more proactive in listening to our soul's calling.

> "Life is never stagnation. It is constant movement, un-rhythmic movement, as we as constant change. Things live by moving and gain strength as they go." Bruce Lee

FIND YOUR TRIBE

The path to realising a life that reflects our essence will sometimes involve finding a group of people who see us for who we are and not who we have been. Re-inventing ourselves whilst in the company of people who keep reminding us of who we *were* may feel comforting, but is not helpful to our evolution. Sometimes even having our closest people relate to us in the same old way may keep us where we are and make it difficult to build our new and improved selves.

As someone who greatly values comfort and enjoys my lifelong relationships, it was painful to realise that talking to the people who I grew up with did not inspire me to take the direction to where I wanted to go. People who are comfortable with what is familiar will not understand why you would want to leap into the unknown. It is not for lack of love but simply the fact that this idea is foreign to them, and therefore scary. An example for many of us is our parents who have dedicated their lives to protecting us. The thought of us paving our way feels to them daunting and unsafe. This added fear and scepticism from those close to us is often paralysing when combined with the doubt that we ourselves may have.

For this reason, it is so important to find a group of like-minded people who have already been to the place you want to go or accomplished what you are hoping to. Because your new tribe only knows you for the ambitions you have now and knows nothing about your former shortcomings or perceived failures, it is easier to accept our upgraded selves in their company. When we spend time with those who have already achieved what we strive for, our mindset and the benchmarks for what is possible shifts. Through our need to belong, we are forced to level up with our new peers without even realising we are doing so. It is this shift that will ultimately guarantee our progress, as well as the support, insight and useful connections we gain.

I recently put out an intention that I would like to be in the company of an individual who already has in her possession all the things I wish to create for myself. Little did I know when I wrote down this desire that the person I was going to meet and spend time with was a public figure who I had admired for a decade. In fact, never in my wildest dreams did I imagine I was going to spend the afternoon with someone so extraordinary and influential. What I took away from this fantastic day was that this individual was not too different from me. She had created an extraordinary level of abundance in all areas of her life with grace, ease, gentleness and integrity, and being in her presence convinced me that I would do the same. After all, we were not so different.

We live in a world where forming a new social network with people who share our ambitions has never been easier. Social media, platforms like Meetup and the rise of shared working spaces, especially in cities like London, make it not only possible to join like-minded groups but also to form our own in case there is not an existing one out there. Since such platforms are accessible in most cities today, let us join a group of people of similar interests or goals and see how much more tangible our path to freedom will become.

> "Find people who make you stand on your tippy-toes to be seen" – Lisa Nichols

OBSERVE WHERE ACTIONS ARE COMING FROM

Successful people talk at great length about the importance of taking action to get to the desired destination. But what I consider to be more significant is the place inside us that has inspired that action. An action inspired by fear, longing or desperation, for example, will often result in an undesired outcome.

Take a heated argument between two people. Irrespective of how hard each person is trying to get their point across, the message gets lost in feelings of resentment as the intention becomes to bring the other around to their point of view, rather than to come to a resolution. If what we say comes from a place of frustration, anger and resentment, regardless of the words we speak or how right we are, our argument with this person will get progressively worse until communication breaks down completely. If, however, we are feeling appreciative of this person and our sole intention is to come to a solution, it is more likely that the argument will be de-escalated before turning into a fight.

As mentioned earlier, it is funny to observe that the things we do not really mind about come to us easier than the things we obsess over and feel pressure about. This is because the intention that hides behind an action is often the key ingredient to determining how the situation will unfold. For example, the difference between confronting a person from a place of love or from a place of resentment may not be explicitly reflected in our words, but it will be communicated to them in other ways. Irrespective of our words, only the true intention of why we are confronting the person will come across. For this reason, we should observe and question the motives behind our interactions. Questions such as: what am I trying to get out of this situation? And more importantly, why am I aiming toward this particular outcome? Observing the intention behind the actions we take helps us to become conscious of what is driving us and whether this is something that needs to be resolved with ourselves or with the other person.

Let us observe where our actions are being inspired from. What is the intention behind each of our actions? Are we doing what we know is right, or are we trying to control a person or a situation? Once we reflect on our actions in this way, it becomes obvious where we are putting our foot wrong and why some circumstances in our lives continue to be a challenge.

THE RULES DO NOT HAVE TO APPLY

The day I began feeling free was the day I realised the rules do not have to apply to me; those I adopted from society, the mainstream, friends, family, popular opinion, and most powerful of all, patterns from my own past experiences. It occurred to me that I was the one who had accepted these rules, and so could just as easily decide to be an exception to every single one of them.

Most of us are not living the joy-filled life that we could be living because our behaviours and beliefs about who we are and how far we could go are limited by a set of arbitrary rules.

The highly successful and inspiring Founder of the female underwear brand Spanx, Sarah Blakely, did not go through the regular channels to get her product into a retailer, which was to attend trade shows and stand around waiting to be discovered. Instead, she found out where the purchasing office was located, drove there, and asked to speak to the head of purchasing who said yes to her product that same day. Instead of following her peers and paying her way into a trade show, Sarah did what she felt was the most direct and simple approach to getting results. The point is this: if we do not ask, we do not get. Had Sarah played by the rules and promoted her product through a particular channel to be noticed, as all her peers did, she never would have taken the simple step of going straight to the purchasing officer and asking for a deal.

Another compelling example that illustrates the arbitrary nature of rules and norms is a successful London-based West end musical actress I recently interviewed for a podcast. What is unique about this individual is that she has been disabled from birth and is one of the only handful of disabled actresses worldwide today, who has made a successful career for herself. Had she done the research and seen the lack of disabled actresses that have made a career in acting, she would have surely been discouraged. In many people's eyes, this wonderful performer, given the statistics, would have been perfectly justified in giving up the dream. Luckily, she chose not to be limited by the rules relating to what it takes to be an actress and has gotten much further than she ever dreamt possible.

My hope is that this chapter helps you to realise that only you get to make up the rules about what's possible for you and the way it will be possible for you. No one else is in charge despite appearances.

Let us think of the thing we want most in our lives and reflect on the rules we have imposed on ourselves that keep us from crossing the bridge to achieve this goal. The point of this exercise is to become conscious and in turn contemplate how, by thinking out of the box, we can eliminate these self-imposed obstacles from hindering our joyful journey.

WHY NOT TELL A FAVOURABLE STORY?

The following chapter further explores our ability to rewrite our circumstances and in turn have our reality conform to this new narrative.

As someone who likes to experiment and play with the idea of shaping my reality, I went through a phase where I told myself uplifting stories about how my life would turn out. While trying to piece myself together following a breakup, I told myself every day that I would not just be fine, but that I would be better and happier than ever before. These words did little to make me feel better in that moment, or even in the days that followed. Even so, I had hit rock bottom, so I was happy to continue telling myself what felt like complete lies.

As time went on, however, my story started to have more and more weight and influence on my state of mind. It was not yet evident in my experience, but I felt comforted and energised in my eventual conviction. I felt the weight lift off my shoulders more each day and slowly my reality started to mirror what previously felt like lies; I discovered a whole new level to the magic that is life.

Had I not fed myself the speech about getting better, it could be argued that I would have come out of the misery eventually anyway; however, I do not believe I would have done so as quickly, easily, and in moments even as joyfully as I did. The stories we tell ourselves about ourselves and our lives matter and are something we should all pay attention to.

My point is this: since we are telling ourselves a story anyway, why not make it an uplifting and joyful one? The probability of our lives turning out to be lame is no more likely than it turning out to be amazing. Whichever option we forecast, we are creating potential non-truths because we do not know how things are going to play out. So, here is a radical idea for you, dear reader, that worked for me time and time again: why not tell yourself the most magical, epic, incredible, dreamy story about your present reality and future that you can think of? Tell the story every day and see how it starts to be reflected in your experience.

Here is your opportunity to write a new narrative for your life.

THE REDUNDANCE OF COMPLAINING

A profound realisation I experienced in my journey as an adult is that complaining is a huge waste of time at best and a heavy (and very unnecessary) liability at worst. Recognising and acknowledging that something is not the way we want it to be is one thing. Taking out valuable time to repeatedly talk about shortcomings is entirely something else. In my thirty-seven years of life, complaining has never once served me.

Tony Robbins and many other star personal development gurus emphasise that 'where attention goes, energy flows.' In no other circumstance does this become more obvious than when we spend lengthy amounts of time talking about the faults we recognise in something or someone. Complaining is detrimental on two fronts; for one, it creates a dead-end where there could otherwise be a simple solution, and secondly, it causes whatever we are complaining about to become more prominent in our experience. While talking openly about what we are feeling is constructive and necessary, my rule is this: if my hating on someone or something turns into more than a single conversation, it is one too many, and it's time to hang up the phone, walk away and put my mentally constructed sword away.

I challenge us all to become acutely aware of how much time we spend having downward spiralling conversations with partners, friends, families and colleagues. These types of conversations typically include criticising, judging, blaming and generally hating on something or someone. As covered in my earlier chapter, it is important to remember that the world does not owe any of us a thing, and therefore no one is liable to live their life by the standards we have set for ourselves.

A wise person once told me that if you feel like the whole world is in the wrong, it is probably just you. Let us reflect on what we are complaining about. Is this an ongoing theme? If it is, then it may not be the other person or the situation that is a problem; instead, there is something in complaining about it that is serving us in some way. Maybe a rant about the terrible state of the economy is a way of excusing ourselves from not looking for a new job and leaving the one we are unhappy in? The bigger question to consider is this: would we even have the time to complain if we were doing something about changing whatever it is we are not happy with? Probably not.

It is a lot easier to criticise, blame and judge our surroundings than it is to make peace with where we are. It is for this reason that not engaging in these types of conversations takes practice, discipline, and may even mean ending certain relationships. It is, however, well worth the sacrifice.

Adversity is a perfectly expected and even necessary part of the human experience. What matters is how we roll with the punches. The idea of this next exercise is to find out whether there is a better way of handling ourselves during these times.

Let us reflect on the last time we went on a rant about something we perceived to be going very wrong in our lives. How many people did we share this news with? How did we feel after the conversation? What was the outcome of this situation? How could it have been handled differently?

CREATE IN YOURSELF THAT WHICH YOU WISH TO SEE IN OTHERS

I once knew a girl who was a magnet for good people and situations. She breezed her way through life laughing and making fun of her journey. She would give compliments to strangers with such overwhelming sincerity that people had no choice but to be charmed. Her presence was always light, and she seemed more fascinated with life than anyone around her. I am sure you too know someone like my friend.

What I learned from her was that our state of mind has the power to colour every single situation we find ourselves in. She so powerfully and sincerely believed that she was the most interesting and interested person in the room, that no matter who she talked to, each person in her presence would walk away thinking the same. Her approach however was never arrogant or forced, but instead curious, fascinated, and childlike – as if she was discovering herself and her surroundings for the first time. What she possessed was the power of wonder.

The ability to influence any situation or person with the certainty and confidence of what we are emitting creates a positive influence on those we interact with. If, for example, you would like to have a fun time with someone who is usually not fun, embody and therefore bring forward the feeling of it in such a way that the other person (irrespective of the mood they are in) has no choice but to conform to the lightness you are putting out. I believe that there is not a situation too overwhelming once we have practiced staying centred in that which we would like to see outside of us.

The ability to make anything we wish to out of a situation may be our greatest power. Once we apply our imagination and at the same time remain loyal and faithful to that innate knowing and peace, we influence everything and everyone around us, and always in a positive way.

I recently talked to my very frazzled and distressed friend who had just come out of a traumatic situation into believing she was brave and in control. I told her how proud I was of her for having enough self-respect to act in the way she had acted. I emphasised how far she had come, how much wiser she was and how bright her future was going to be. Whilst empathising with her situation, I chose to see the powerful person in her instead of the vulnerable hopeless one she was showing me. The result of projecting my positive and empowered perspective onto her resulted in her recounting all the things she had done correctly over the past few months. She regained her composure and acted like the person I knew her to be. The shift in her mindset proved to me once again how powerful we can be when we remain centred in our conviction and project that positive image onto others.

Let us put this into practice by seeing the very best in the person we next interact with. Spend half an hour beforehand reflecting on how they are special and everything that we cherish about the relationship. This will likely result in a joyful interaction where we witness all the positive attributes of this person reflected back to us .

THE POWER OF FREE GENEROSITY

In the following chapter, I would like to zone in on one characteristic my friend in the previous section exuded that made her so magnetic: generosity. If I could sum up greatness in a human in one single characteristic, it would be this willingness to contribute to others without the need for anything in return.

When I think of the people I look up to most and would not hesitate to do anything for, they all have this one attribute in common. They are generous in all ways, but most of all with their spirit. When in the presence of others, they give of themselves freely and always contribute immensely to every interaction. They show up with high energy and an intention to uplift the other person or group, whether they be close friends, family members or a complete stranger. They show this by giving a small gift of appreciation, always offering encouragement, making others laugh or simply showing interest and curiosity for another person's experience.

I previously mentioned that I sense we are all here to contribute something to the world. In many ways, the exercises in this text aim to encourage vigilant self-care so that we are able to give freely, generously and abundantly, without depleting our own reservoir. The act of giving our presence and attention strengthens us individually and collectively in ways that cannot be quantified or contained. Whether we affect millions of people with our contribution or are a rainbow in the life of one other person (as my favourite poet Maya Angelou says) is irrelevant. When we give freely of ourselves in any way, it causes a ripple effect that is equally compelling.

Conversely what I have observed in others who are closed off, miserable and frustrated in their life is that they lack generosity. They are always on the defence about being taken for granted and as a result give very little of themselves. In this way, they perpetuate the sense of loneliness they feel.

If there was ever a quick-fix remedy for someone who is in this state, I would prescribe they take a few hours out of their own (usually) self-consumed lives to make someone else's life better. In my own experience, the act of giving has been healing and restorative. Knowing someone feels better and more confident because of something I did for them is empowering and provides space from whatever is bothering me. For this reason, being generous is an act of both selfishness and selflessness.

Further, generosity is more than just a gesture towards another. It is also a way of showing respect for life and appreciation for all the gifts one has been given. To freely share ourselves generously and give back to life as it gives to us, provides a baseline for an abundant and joy-filled life because whatever we give will come back. Known to the west as the zen millionaire, Japanese author Ken Honda shares an experiment he did to test this theory by sending out free copies of his book by mailing them out himself. What resulted from this generous act was a second book deal which sold seven million copies worldwide.

Being generous is a ritual I take very seriously in my own day to day life. Whenever in the presence of anyone I have chosen to spend time with, I am intentional about being fully present and make sure they know they matter. I also love to send notes on

Instagram to strangers whose page inspires me to let them know I appreciate their work. It only takes ten minutes out of my day but could be all the encouragement someone needs to move forward. Whether we have little or a lot to give is irrelevant, so long as we are intentional about making this a regular part of our daily routine.

I hope that by this point, you are feeling fuller of yourself and more inspired to be alive. If so, let us make it a daily practice to give the best of ourselves. It could be as simple as smiling as you walk past a stranger, being more present to your colleague as they tell you about their weekend or taking your favourite person out for dinner- Just because. You will notice immediately how much your own mood improves and in turn your act may be just the thing that makes someone else's day.

Use the space below to think of ways you can make a ritual out of being more generous in small or big ways.

THE SECRET OF NATURE IS HER PATIENCE

When we look at nature, we notice how effortlessly it evolves from one thing to another. A tree, for example, does not wonder where its nourishment will come from or doubt its evolution. It does not fear its death or live in the future, nor does it worry about the past. I suspect this is the reason we crave spending time in nature and are almost immediately uplifted in its presence. Something about its peaceful existence mirrors a significant part in us.

Realising we are all part of nature's mystical cycle should encourage us as humans to be more like this. In practical terms, this means to worry less and enjoy more, laugh at the perceived challenges, and not take it all so seriously or personally. As Russell Brand so poignantly remarked, "we'll all soon be dead".

Remember Coelho's words: when we know what we want, the whole universe conspires to assist us in that journey. Whatever your religion or spiritual beliefs, I believe that we have all deep down experienced the truth in this. Let us be more like nature and be certain that when we are nourished from the inside by remaining true to our inner calling, we inevitably grow into that which we are supposed to be.

Remember, the journey to whatever your definition of success is, does not need to be a difficult one, but it will demand that you remain stubbornly focused, yet also playful and filled with peace every step of the way.

CONSCIOUSLY SEEK OUT HUMOUR IN UNFORTUNATE CIRCUMSTANCES

With a little help from our imagination, it is possible to see the humour in just about every mundane situation in this strange journey we call life. When we make a conscious decision to divorce ourselves from our experience and look at ourselves as a character in our own movie, we can become the observer of our human self in its interaction with its environment. This unlikely shift in perspective has seen me remain completely calm, centred and often amused at my predicaments (when I probably should have been losing my mind). Between not knowing whether to laugh or cry, I always chose to laugh.

Just like every other practice, this one also takes consistent reinforcement. But once it becomes second nature, life becomes an amusing comedy of which you are the star. Let us think back to the last time we watched a character in a comedy finding themselves in an uncomfortable situation and how amused we were to watch them struggling in their predicament. Now let us make that character ourselves, for the rest of time.

TAKE THE SCARY OPTION

Much of this text is focused on one key outcome: to shift our perspective on what is possible for our life. When looking back on what has made the most impact on shattering my own limiting beliefs, I conclude that it has been taking the scary option. Each time I have chosen a path that was uncertain but exciting, I experienced a significant shift in my perception of what is possible. Researchers of epigenetics and metaphysics might say that I experienced a quantum leap. This is where my perception of myself shifted so significantly, that I no longer felt like the same person I was the week or even the day before. To truly convince our body that we are ready for an extraordinary life and cast aside our perceived limitations, we must take risks that put us in a place we have not yet been. The more often we do this, the more open we become to a significant change in our circumstances.

While affirmations may slowly condition us out of our limiting beliefs, they do not compare to the speedy impact of moving forward in the face of fear and uncertainty. As Richard Branson wisely points out, if someone offers you an opportunity and you are not sure you can do it, say yes, and learn how to do it later. We may not always reach the goal we are aiming for, but we will be sure to learn something along the way that will help us go all the way the next time around.

On my recent trip to Norway, I decided to give skiing a try for the first time since I was a child. Despite the moderately steep slope they insisted was the beginners' hill, I decided not to get an instructor and to figure it out myself. During my climb up, however, I felt a nagging panic settle in my stomach. Suddenly, the hill looked much steeper than it did from the bottom. Still, I kept walking up until I reached the top of it. By this stage, I was in full-blown panic mode. After carefully sliding myself off from the top, I quickly picked up speed and the only thing I could do was turn my feet inward to try and slow myself down. Despite my best efforts, I raced ahead and eventually had no choice but throw myself into the snow to stop myself from continuing at the terrifying speed I was going. I was in shock as I stared in horror at my awkwardly bent knee. Every cell in my body felt like quitting and joining my friends who had opted for cross country skiing instead. However, I did not take my skis off that day. Instead, I made friends with the crippling fear and decided I was going to figure this out. I knew how to slow myself down and throw myself sideways and that was good enough for me. After many falls and some slight bruising, I was exhausted. However, something amazing happened: I was able to ski to the bottom of the hill without killing myself or anyone else on the track. That day, I started to refer to myself differently. I became the person who had made friends with my fear and would not let it stand in my way. I had proven to myself that I was braver than my mind had allowed me to believe. Since then, I have been unqualified for most projects I have taken on but have somehow managed to find my way in the dark. Steep learning curves have since become a regular part of my life journey.

Let us reflect on and write down what it would mean to step out of our comfort zone now. This can come in any form imaginable. It could be a message to someone that you have been putting off writing for fear of the response, or perhaps it's developing a skill like public speaking. Anything that gives us that slightly sick feeling in the stomach but is accompanied by butterflies of excitement in our stomach is an activity worth taking on.

Once the list is complete, let us commit to putting ourselves in an unfamiliar situation, even if we must do so in the face of fear and resistance. Unfortunately, there is no end to this exercise. For life to become everything we want it to be, becoming friends with our fear must become a lifestyle in a never-ending quest to get past our limits.

LEARN TO FALL WELL

Apart from realising how stubborn I was, another very important takeaway I gained from my attempt to ski in Norway was the importance of learning to fall well. The main reason I did not hit a tree or a child on the way down the hill was that I had worked out I could throw myself into the snow on my side in a way that was not going to break any bones. This is an important metaphor for life. If you have lived enough by the time you pick up this text, you will know that falls are inevitable. Just like none of us get out alive, not one of us gets to have a smooth ride while we are here either. What is important is to learn to fall in a way that will ensure the damage of the impact is minimal to our lifeforce.

Just like everything else, this is a balancing act that takes practice and focus. How long should we mourn a broken relationship? How much time should we work on healing past traumas? These are age-old questions and there are no straightforward answers. However, four mind tricks have kept me going so far. Here they are:

1. Training myself to turn every negative situation around in a way that I can extract some benefit, no matter how small. The trick is to focus all the energy I have left on that small benefit.

2. Changing the way I look at an undesired experience by widening my perspective on it. This is done by asking questions such as, will this matter in three months' time?

How is this situation funny? Who else do I know who this has happened to and how did they deal with it?

3. The third tool is my relentless belief that no matter how it looks, life always knows best, and things always work out. No exceptions. The ability to react to every negative situation in this way takes determination, focus and repeating affirmations that we may not necessarily believe are true in the moment. However, the more we practise, the more of a default this reaction becomes.

4. Lastly, always reminding myself that there is an order to the cosmos that has a way of bringing all things into perfect balance, irrespective of our interference or preference. We are all subject to this ever-present process of balance and rebalance in a way that makes life just and equal (even though, on the surface, it often seems that the very opposite is true).

There are situations in life, such as the death of a loved one, where the above tools will be less effective, if effective at all. The process of grieving is incredibly intense and overwhelming. There are not many words anyone could put on paper to try and help with this process. What I do know is that for most situations, the above tools can work for you too and perhaps the better we get at handling the small hurdles, the better equipped we will be to fall better when hitting the big ones.

THE WORLD IS AS YOU ARE – ASSUME EVERYTHING IS A REFLECTION OF YOURSELF

The idea that "the world is as we are" is an important one to adopt in what has hopefully become our intentional life journey. When we look back at our experiences, it is useful to reflect on our beliefs, mood and state of mind at the time that this situation occurred. Our mindset dictated how we experienced the situation. In the same way, to change our circumstances, we must change our state of mind first.

A way to think of this is by looking at our reflection in the mirror. When we blame our external circumstances, it is like blaming our reflection in the mirror for frowning when we frown or smiling when we smile. The reflection has no will of its own and is merely responding to the expression we chose to make. So are the circumstances in our life: nothing more than a manifested form of what is happening inside our internal world.

To accept responsibility for everything that happens to us as either a conscious choice or a manifestation of our positive or negative beliefs can seem unfair, as it may appear that life is happening to us. However, adopting this perspective sets ourselves free from life's ups and downs. Owning every experience as one we created, whether the responsibility lies completely with us or not, empowers us to change what we see, in the same way we would smile if we wish to see ourselves smiling back in the mirror.

An example which illustrates this principle was a trip I took to a country everyone had warned me about. I was told people were bitter, unfriendly, unsmiling, and unaccommodating. What was convincing about this narrative was that I was hearing the stories predominantly from people who were from this country. However, before getting there, I reminded myself that the world is as I am and that if I go there in full faith that people would be lovely and welcoming, then, so it would be. Not surprisingly, this was exactly what I experienced. Not only was every person I interacted with warm and welcoming, but I even got invited to a couple of parties in the few days I was there. People smiled on the street and were friendly and helpful the entire time. This proved to me, once again, that no matter what everyone tells us about stereotypes and their own impressions, our experience has all the potential in the world to be our own because we get to decide how we show up in it, and this in turn is what will shape the proceeding circumstances.

To put this theory into practice, let us think of a situation in our life that does not live up to our preferences. Now write down your desired version of the situation. Provided we approach this exercise from a playful and relaxed state of mind, we can immediately notice ideas that start to flow to us about how this situation may be open to change, and the alternatives and perspectives which had not dawned on us before. This exercise unlocks us from the undesired circumstance we find ourselves in and opens us up to ways in which we can change it to our desired outcome.

FINAL WORDS

The universe will only support the real you. If there was one way to summarise this entire text into one sentence, it would be this simple statement. The universe, God, higher self, inner being, the wild self, however you want to call it – has never supported a false self and it never will. Simply being ourselves is a message that should have been wedged in our minds by age five by parents, caregivers, teachers, older siblings, aunties, uncles, and everyone else we came in contact with. The real self is our very essence, the knowing that is forever ours, the wild self who I hope you have felt surfacing while reading this text and participating in the exercises.

It is only when we decide to honour our truth and recognise our innate worth that this will be reflected in our experience. Everything else will be a rehearsal for the real bliss that life has the potential to be. When I decided to move to London, I was well trained in this lesson. I did not worry about starting from scratch and how I would go about building a satisfying life, because I knew every cell in my body was on board with this decision. This state of mind proved more powerful than months of meticulous planning. I had no budget, no plan, no place to stay and no job. What I did have was the absolute conviction that I was going to be ok, and so I truly was.

My first few days in London were spent in a beautiful Airbnb where a guest of the host dropped in unexpectedly and gave me the contact of a girl who was looking for a housemate in Notting Hill, one of my favourite parts of the city. I found myself a few days later speed walking down Ledbury Road feeling ecstatic with excitement in knowing I was likely going to be calling this majestic street my new home. Things only got better from there. My new flatmate offered that I move in straight away without the worry of paying a deposit or any sort of paperwork to complicate or delay the process. The flat was by no means my dream home, but it had more character and charm than most places I had called home before.

Just like that, my new residence in my favourite city was sorted with no flat hunting and no dealing with agents – in fact, not a single minute was spent trying to find it because it had found me before I even had the chance to start looking. Around the same week, I received an email from a recruitment agent for an application I had sent so long ago when I was back in Australia that I did not even remember making it. I went in the next day and got the job.

Things continued to fall into my lap just as I believed they would. My housemates were an interesting and funny duo who kept me well entertained and taken care of for my first few months in London. The job at the university made me so miserable that it prompted me to write this text. And so, little did I know at the time, it was the beginning of the end of my Monday to Friday grind, which I discovered had never been part of my true self.

More than ever, I am convinced that those of us who remain true to our spirit are more powerful than the millions who do not. Today, my claim to success is that I feel like the most blessed person alive most of the time. I am present in the moment and have no impulse to think about what is going to happen the following week or even the following day. That said, my quest to stay true to my consistently evolving self in all areas of my life is a work in progress. I have written this text to remind myself of this, as much as I hope it will help you in recognising that no matter where you find yourself in life, you can always come back to the truth of who you are.

My hope, dear readers, is that I have inspired the wild child, the dreamer, the eternal optimist and the God part of you that was never absent, but merely sleeping and very much alive.

Finally, I will leave you all with these words from Bentinho Massaro:

"You, who walk in confidence in your highest intention – devoid of expectation and appreciative of every moment regardless of how it appears to unfold – will walk this universe with unshakable truth and unfettered tread.

To you, mountains will move, oceans shall part, trees will bow down, and lions shall sleep on your lap.

You have emptied your fears, revealed yourself as infinite and have gone where no illusion can grab hold. Thus, you remain free of misery and vastly beyond the ability to despair.

You have discovered the secret to freedom. The spear that pierces all veils of dis-ease. You have become courage itself.

To you I bow down and say this: against all odds and despite endless levels of ignorance being thrown your way, you chose to listen only to the truth and remain utterly doubtless about it, no matter the consequences. From the far end of the spectrum of illusion and the way here to the truth and beyond, you've made it back and I rejoice! Welcome home."

BIBLIOGRAPHY/REFERENCE LIST

Women who run with the Wolves, Clarissa Pinkola Estes, 2008, UK, Rider Publishing
The Power of Myth, Joseph Campbell and Bill Moyers, 1988, Betty Sue Flowers (ed.). New York: Doubleday
Ask and it is Given: Learning to Manifest Your Desires, Esther and Jerry Hicks, 2004, Hay House Publishing
The Alchemist, Paulo Coelho, 1988, Harper Torch Publishing
You Are the Placebo, Joe Dispenza, 2014, UK, Hay House Publishing
The Hero's way Post-2017, Bentinho Massaro
Notes on a nervous planet, Matt Haig, 2018, Canongate Books

RECOMMENDED READING LIST

The four agreements by Don Miguel Ruiz
The Artist's Way by Julia Cameron
You Are the Placebo, Becoming Supernatural by Dr Joe Dispenza
Ask and it is Given: Learning to Manifest Your Desires by Esther and Jerry Hicks
Women who run with the Wolves by Clarissa Pinkola Estes
Veronica Decides to Die by Paolo Coelho
The Power of Now by Eckhart Tolle
*The Subtle Art of Not Giving a F*CK* by Mark Manson
The monk who sold his Ferrari by Robin Sharma
Happy Money by Ken Honda

ABOUT THE AUTHOR

Gia Lulic lives in west London and is a writer and creative in multiple disciplines. Her drive is to convince others of the innate power they can unlock in themselves and awaken those around her to the magic that is this life experience. Most of her time is spent listening to experts on the theme and experimenting with these principles in her day-to-day life. Gia enjoys her life in London and views it as a rich playground, and a consistent source of inspiration for her craft. She strives to make her own life the best example of one lived with ease and joy and to inspire others to do the same.

Follow Gia @the_girl_loves_london

Printed in Great Britain
by Amazon

41721329R00086